OUR WORLD OUR FUTURE

Protecting Wildlife

Sharon Dalgleish

CHELSEA HOUSE
PUBLISHERS
A Haights Cross Communications ● Company
Philadelphia

This edition first published in 2003 in the United States of America by Chelsea House Publishers, a subsidiary of Haights Cross Communications.

Reprinted 2004

Chelsea House Publishers
1974 Sproul Road, Suite 400
Broomall, PA 19008-0914

The Chelsea House world wide web address is www.chelseahouse.com

Library of Congress Cataloging-in-Publication Data Applied for.
ISBN 0-7910-7021-2

First published in 2002 by
MACMILLAN EDUCATION AUSTRALIA PTY LTD
627 Chapel Street, South Yarra, Australia, 3141

Edited by Sally Woollett
Text design by Karen Young
Cover design by Karen Young
Page layout and simple diagrams by Nina Sanadze
Technical illustrations and maps by Pat Kermode, Purple Rabbit Productions

Printed in China

Acknowledgements
Cover photograph: Giant panda in the Wolong Reserve, China, courtesy of Jean-Paul Ferrero/Auscape.

ANT Photo Library, p. 9 (bottom); Derek Bromhall-OSF/Auscape, p. 24 (bottom); Jean-Paul Ferrero/Auscape, pp. 13 (right), 17 (bottom); Dan Guravich—OSF/Auscape, p. 11 (right); D. Parer & E. Parer-Cook/Auscape, p. 15 (bottom); Doug Perrine/Auscape, p. 17 (top); Robyn Stewart/Auscape, p. 6 (bottom right); Steve Turner/Auscape, p. 19 (top); Australian Picture Library/Corbis, p. 24 (top); Coo-ee Picture Library, pp. 10, 11 (left), 20 (top); The DW Stock Picture Library, pp. 4 (top left, top center, top right and bottom left), 14, 18 (top), 20 (bottom), 25 (top and bottom) (broccoli, kale, brussels sprouts, cauliflower and kohlrabi); Victor Englebert, pp. 6 (top, center left, center right and bottom left), 12 (bottom), 22, 23; Getty Images/ Photodisc, pp. 4 (bottom center), 30; Denis Crawford/Graphic Science, p. 8; Imageaddict.com, pp. 4 (bottom right), 7 (center and right); © 2001 Mark A. Johnson, pp. 7 (left), 21; Legend Images, p. 25 (cabbage); Jiri Lochman/Lochman Transparencies, p. 16 (right); Alex Steffe/Lochman Transparencies, p. 15 (top); photolibrary.com, p. 13 (left); Terry Oakley/The Picture Source, p. 16 (left); Southern Images/Silkstone, p. 18 (bottom); Mark Edwards/Still Pictures, p. 29 (bottom); Michael Gunther/Still Pictures, p. 19 (bottom); Geoff Murray/Tasmanian Photo Library, p. 6 (center); World Images, pp. 9 (top), 12 (top), 29 (top); World Wide Fund For Nature, p. 28.

Contents

READ MORE ABOUT:

Look out for this box. It will tell you the other pages in this book where you can find out more about related topics.

Our world

We are connected to everything in our world. We are connected through the air we breathe, the water we drink, the food we eat, the energy we use, and the soil we live on.

To keep our world healthy, all these elements must work together.

water

land

energy

wildlife

forests

air

SHOW ME

The parts of your body work together to keep you healthy. If one part of your body stops working properly, you get sick!

Our future

The number of people in our world is now doubling every 40 years. This means that when you are grown up there could be twice as many people on Earth as there are now.

Every person on Earth needs certain things to survive. We need to make sure our world will still be able to give people everything they need to live, now and in the future.

▲ Now.

▲ Forty years from now.

STOP & THINK

Suppose that one part of our world were to stop working properly. What do you think might happen to the rest of our world?

5

Different worlds

Our world supports an amazing number of environments. There are hot deserts, windy mountains, tropical rainforests, grasslands, evergreen forests, freezing Arctic and Antarctic regions, deep oceans and flowing rivers. Different **species** of plants and animals have found ways to live in these environments.

▲ People have found ways to live in the desert.

▲ Some animals are well suited to mountain climates.

▲ Many species of plants and animals live in the rainforests.

▲ Giraffes can eat the vegetation that grows in grasslands.

▲ These palm trees can grow in the salty and windy conditions near the ocean.

▲ Polar bears hunt for food in the icy waters of the Arctic.

SHOW ME

The town or city you live in is part of your environment. If you move to a new town, sometimes you have to change the way you do things.

Links in the chain

Each of the environments in our world is called an ecosystem. In an ecosystem, the land, water, plants and animals are all connected by food chains.

grass ———→ eaten by ———→ zebra ———→ eaten by ———→ lion

The plants and animals in a food chain need each other for survival. Look at the food chain on this page. If hunters kill the lions, there will be more zebras because there will be fewer lions left to eat them. But all these extra zebras will eat more grass. Soon there will be no grass left to eat. Then the zebras will die, too.

Some animals are part of a number of food chains. They eat, or are eaten by, a number of different animals. All these food chains linked together are called a food web. Everything in a food web works together. Changing one part of a web affects every other part.

STOP & THINK
How can we make sure these ecosystems (including our own) keep working?

If a single plant species becomes extinct, up to 40 animals that depend on it might also be threatened.

The variety of life

No one knows exactly how many different species of plants and animals live in our world. So far, scientists have found and named about 2.5 million. There could be millions more that have not yet been discovered. There is a word for this huge variety of different life—biodiversity. *Bio* means "life." *Diversity* means "difference."

In 1997 scientists found 16,000 species of wildlife that had never before been recorded—all in one cave in Spain.

Biodiversity helps keep each ecosystem, and our whole world, in balance. The more diversity in an ecosystem, the better chance the ecosystem has to survive. This is because any damage that does happen in the food web has a better chance of being balanced somewhere else in the web.

▶ There are more than 900,000 species of insects, all with different shapes, sizes and colors.

STOP & THINK
Do all things have a right to live, whether they are useful to you or not?

Dying species

Since 1950 we have been losing species at a faster rate than ever before. Between 50 and 100 species of plants and animals around our world become extinct every day. That is more in one day than we used to lose in 100 years. Ecosystems that were once rich in species are turning into deserts or unnatural, human-made environments.

Most of this damage is caused because of the increase in the number of people living in our world and the way of life of people living in **developed countries**. People are killing plants and animals, or destroying their **habitats**, up to 10,000 times faster than ever before. This is affecting biodiversity and disturbing the natural balance. In the future, there will be fewer species of plants and animals for us to live with.

A species is said to be **extinct** if it has not been seen for 50 years. Dinosaurs became extinct 65 million years ago. Today, one-eighth of all plant species are threatened with extinction.

▲ Natural meadows such as this one filled with wildflowers, insects and spiders are now rare in Europe. More than 6,000 species of European insects are facing extinction.

▶ There are only about 300 Siberian tigers left in the wild. Every year their home in the Russian mountains gets warmer and wetter. By 2010 their habitat could be suitable for farming. If the land is cleared to grow crops, where will the Siberian tigers live?

READ MORE ABOUT:

- food webs on page 7
- habitats on pages 12 and 14
- biodiversity on page 24.

SHOW ME

Go outside and collect as many different leaves as you can. If you have a garden, look there. Look along the street where you live. Look in any nearby park. How many different leaves did you collect? The more you collected, the richer the diversity where you live!

A change in the weather

The amount of **carbon dioxide** in the air today is one-third higher than it was 200 years ago. Part of the reason is that we are cutting down more trees. Trees and green plants take in carbon dioxide from the air and use it to make their food.

Not only are we cutting down more trees, at the same time we are pumping more carbon dioxide out of cars, factories and power stations. The trees that are left cannot take in all of the carbon dioxide being made.

All this carbon dioxide stays in the atmosphere and acts like a sheet of glass on a greenhouse. It lets the sunlight through but does not let all the heat back out—just like inside a real greenhouse.

This greenhouse effect keeps Earth much warmer than it would otherwise be. Without it, our world would be covered in ice. The problem is that when there is too much carbon dioxide, it traps too much heat. Then the world gets even warmer.

Scientists think this warmer weather—called global warming—will change the weather patterns in our world. There will be more floods, storms, droughts, hurricanes and other unusual weather.

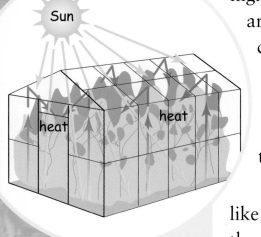

▲ Greenhouses are used mainly in cold countries. The heat trapped inside helps the flowers and vegetables grow.

▶ Global warming could change the weather.

STOP & THINK
Will climate changes affect wildlife?

In hot water

Even a small change in climate can affect an ecosystem. Many plants and animals will die because they will not be able to live in the new weather conditions. Others, such as cockroaches and mosquitoes, will do very well in the warmer weather and move into ecosystems that were previously too cold for them.

▲ Polar bears in Canada are getting sick and dying. The warmer weather is causing the winter ice to break earlier. The bears must move off the ice and onto land, where there is less food for them to eat.

► Warmer seas are destroying coral reefs. The hottest sea temperatures ever were recorded in 1998. Every coral reef ecosystem in the world was affected. It could take 100 years for the reefs to recover.

YOU CAN DO iT!

🐾 Most electricity is made by burning **fossil fuels**. Fossil fuels release carbon dioxide into the air. Save as much electricity as you can around the house. Here are some ways you can do it:

🐾 Turn lights off when you leave a room.

🐾 Ask your parents to buy energy-saving lightbulbs. Tell them they cost more to buy—but they also last a lot longer!

🐾 Do not leave televisions, stereos and computers on when you are not using them.

🐾 Cars run on fossil fuels, so do not ask your parents to drive you places when you could easily and safely walk.

Paving over habitats

As the number of people in our world grows, we need more land to build our homes, more farmland to grow our food, and more **raw materials** to make useful and fun things to fill our homes. We can only get these resources by taking habitats from wildlife. When a plant or animal loses its habitat, it dies.

Wetlands are areas where rivers, lakes or seas meet the land. They support great biodiversity. Rich plant life grows in the shallow water covering the land. This swampy area provides the ideal breeding ground for small creatures, which in turn feed many species of fish, **amphibians**, insects, birds and mammals. About half the world's wetlands are gone forever. They have been drained so that the land can be paved over for buildings. Other habitats have been destroyed by digging mines and damming rivers.

▲ The raw materials to make all the things we like to buy come from the land. This habitat has been destroyed by careless mining. No wildlife can live here.

▶ People use huge amounts of water. A lot of the water we use is stored in **reservoirs** made by building a dam across a river. When a reservoir is created, habitats are flooded. This land in Africa used to be covered in forest and filled with wildlife.

STOP & THINK
How can people balance their need for land and **resources** with the needs of plants and animals for natural habitats?

Bring back the wild

Some people have realized that all habitats are important to the balance in our world. They are trying to find ways to save wildlife before it is too late. In 1997 new laws were introduced in the United States to protect wetlands. But wetlands are still disappearing at an alarming rate every year. Other countries have begun replanting trees and creating new habitats for wildlife.

◄ In North America, some of the conifer forests cleared for timber are being replanted. The trees grow straight and fast. This is good news for global warming because the growing trees take in large amounts of carbon dioxide. But the new forests do not have as rich a variety of plants as the old forests.

▲ Giant pandas are in danger. They have lost half their bamboo forest habitat in the mountains of China. The forest is being cleared to make way for farmland. The Chinese government has created forest reserves, such as the Wolong Reserve, to try and save the panda. The small reserves are linked by corridors of trees so the pandas can move between them.

YOU CAN DO IT!

- 🐾 Do not ride trail bikes or drive off-road vehicles in natural areas.
- 🐾 Do not pick or dig up wild plants or flowers.
- 🐾 Plant a garden in your school playground to attract wildlife.
- 🐾 Save water so we do not need to build so many dams.
- 🐾 Before you buy something, think about the raw materials it took to make it and where those raw materials came from. Is it worth it? Do you really need to buy it? Only buy it if the answer is "yes."
- 🐾 Adopt an endangered plant or animal **indigenous** to your local area. Find out how you can help protect it.

READ MORE ABOUT:

- biodiversity on page 8
- global warming on page 10
- habitats on page 14.

Polluting habitats

Mines, factories, power stations and vehicles produce chemicals as waste. Getting rid of this waste can harm wildlife habitats. The chemicals can hang around and be dangerous for hundreds, even thousands, of years.

Many farmers also use chemicals. They use **fertilizers** to make crops grow. They use **pesticides** to stop insects from eating crops. These chemicals also go onto the soil and can run off into nearby rivers.

The waste that does not break down in nature is dangerous. Trees drop millions of leaves every year, but leaves are biodegradable. This means they rot and go slowly into the soil. Many chemicals and plastics are not biodegradable. They do not rot in the soil. They stay in the soil and poison it and the whole food chain. A lot of waste products can end up in waterways.

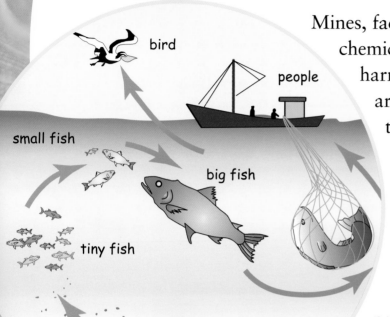

bird
people
small fish
big fish
tiny fish
pollution

▲ This food chain begins in the sea. The poisonous chemicals that are in tiny amounts at the bottom of this food chain collect as they move up the chain. By the time the poison reaches the animal at the top of the chain, that animal will have much more of the poison in its body than the animal at the bottom.

▶ Pesticides used by faraway farmers have been found in the bodies of penguins in Antarctica.

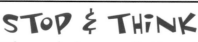

STOP & THINK
If people keep polluting plant and animal habitats, what will happen to the wildlife?

Stop the waste

Coral reefs are important to our world. They take up only a tiny part of the ocean floor, yet they are home to one-quarter of marine species. More than one-quarter of the world's reefs have been killed by pollution from **sewage**, fertilizers and other wastes. The death of the coral affects the rest of the food chains that depend on it for survival. Some scientists think these underwater coral forests may all die out in 20 years.

Wildlife can also be harmed by oil spills and by garbage thrown into waterways.

In many countries, there are now laws so companies that pour wastewater into rivers can be fined. Polluted rivers are also being cleaned up so that fish and other wildlife will return.

▲ Coral reefs have been called the rainforests of the sea.

▼ Plastic waste kills up to one million sea birds, 100,000 sea mammals and countless fish each year. This sea lion on the Galapagos Islands has become entrapped in a discarded plastic bucket.

YOU CAN DO IT!

🐾 Try not to buy goods brought in from another country. Fewer ships carrying goods around the world will mean fewer oil spills.

🐾 Join a volunteer group and clean up a local beach, river, park or other wildlife area.

🐾 If you have a garden, persuade your parents not to use chemical pesticides and fertilizers.

🐾 Never pour paint, oil or chemicals down the drain. Drains lead to rivers and seas.

🐾 Save water. The less water you use, the less wastewater will find its way back into the ocean.

🐾 Recycle as much as you can. If there is less waste to deal with overall we will have more time and resources to work out ways of dealing with dangerous waste.

READ MORE ABOUT:

• food chains on page 7

• habitats on page 12.

Fishing or overfishing?

The number of people living in our world is growing by 90 million people a year. To feed all these hungry people, we need more and more food. Some of this food comes from the sea. In 1950, 23 million tons (21 million metric tons) of fish were taken from the sea. Today more than 110 million tons (100 million metric tons) are taken every year. New fishing methods make it much easier to find and catch fish.

▲ Modern fishing methods use huge fishing nets and electronic equipment.

▲ A driftnet reaches 50 feet (15 meters) into the sea and is 40 miles (65 kilometers) long. It can catch millions of fish at a time. Driftnets also trap dolphins, seals, turtles and birds. These creatures are thrown back into the sea but they are usually injured and die.

STOP & THINK
Who is responsible for the deep oceans and open seas?

An empty ocean

People are catching too many fish and leaving too few behind to breed. This is called overfishing. Some countries have laws limiting the amount of fish that can be caught each year. Some have also banned driftnets in waters close to their coastline. But driftnets are still used in waters far out at sea. These waters are not controlled by any one country and are hard to watch.

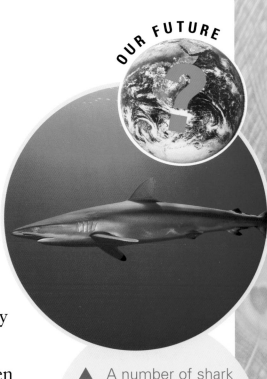

Overfishing can also disturb the natural balance between the different types of fish in the ocean. Sharks are an important part of ocean food chains. For example, if there are fewer great white sharks, seal numbers will grow. More seals will mean fewer numbers of many other fish species.

▲ A number of shark species are in danger. Many are killed illegally just for their fins. The fins are cut off to make shark fin soup and the sharks are left to die.

Whaling has been banned by most countries in our world. Some countries say they need to hunt and kill whales for scientific research. But, once the research is done, the whalers earn money selling the whale meat for food.

▲ Environment groups such as Greenpeace have been trying to save the whales.

YOU CAN DO IT!

🐾 If you eat less meat, you will save fish and other creatures that get caught in fishing nets. One-third of our world's fish catch is used to feed farm animals!

🐾 Buy tuna that has "dolphin friendly" on the can. Many dolphins die when they get trapped in some kinds of tuna fishing nets.

🐾 Every year more than 200 million fish from tropical coral reefs are caught and sold as aquarium fish. Only buy aquarium fish you know have not come from an endangered area.

READ MORE ABOUT:

• food chains on page 7.

Souvenirs and trophies

Early people hunted animals only for food or for fur to make clothes they needed for their survival. Today, animals are hunted for their skins, tusks and horns to make unnecessary things such as tourist souvenirs and luxury goods. In some areas, laws have been made to stop this practice. Many endangered animals are now also protected by law. Still, the animals are not safe. People continue to kill them illegally.

Plants are not safe either. Some people collect rare plants, even in places where this is against the law. They take orchids from rainforests in Asia and cactuses from the deserts of the United States.

▲ Some people will pay a lot of money for products made from tiger bone and other rare-animal parts. Tigers are protected in India but one is still killed every day by **poachers**. In the last 100 years, our world has lost nine out of every ten surviving tigers. If poaching does not stop, tigers will be extinct within the next ten years.

▶ Cactuses are sometimes taken from the desert.

STOP & THINK
Would you rather live in a world rich with different life or a human-made desert?

Greed or need?

It is not always human greed that is the problem. It can also be need. In parts of Africa, people eat and trade in bush meat. Sometimes this includes endangered wild animals. But bush meat is an important source of food and money in areas struggling to survive because of poverty and hunger. Any answers to the problem cannot ignore the needs of these people. The challenge for the future is to allow better living standards for people without losing plant and animal species.

▶ If we are not careful, these horns and skins might be all that is left of some wildlife.

YOU CAN DO iT!

🐾 Do not buy souvenirs made from bird feathers, ivory or furs.

🐾 Be an informed **consumer**. Before buying anything made from coral or shell, ask if it comes from a legal and **sustainable** source.

🐾 If you have a garden, make sure your parents do not buy plants taken from the wild.

🐾 Find out if there is a local wildlife group that needs your help.

🐾 Sometimes the only way to save a species is to breed it in zoos. Then it can be put back in its natural habitat. Visit a local zoo and see what they are doing to help conserve wildlife.

▲ In Africa, elephants are hunted for their ivory tusks and rhinoceroses for their horns. This wildlife guard has **tranquilized** a wild rhino and is sawing off its horn. Without the horn, the animal is worthless to poachers. The guards hope that by doing this they can save rhino lives.

Alien invasion

When a species of plant or animal is introduced to a place it has not lived in before, it is called an alien, exotic or introduced species. Alien species can turn an ecosystem into a disaster area. Because they are not a natural part of the ecosystem, they often have no natural **predators** in the food web. They can reproduce and take over the whole area unchecked.

Sometimes aliens have been introduced on purpose by people to control another type of pest. Sometimes the alien itself can not only control the existing pest, but become a pest itself. It can compete with indigenous wildlife for food or eat the wildlife.

▲ Farmers introduced the South American cane toad into Australia in 1935 to eat beetles that were destroying the sugar cane crops. The toads did a great job and had soon eaten all the beetles. Then they moved on to indigenous insects, fish, birds and small mammals. The cane toads have no natural enemies to keep their numbers under control.

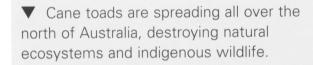

▼ Cane toads are spreading all over the north of Australia, destroying natural ecosystems and indigenous wildlife.

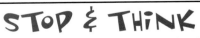

STOP & THINK
Does it matter if aliens take over?

Traveling the world

People travel today more than ever before. This makes it easier for plants and animals to travel, too. People buy **imported** plants for their gardens and imported animals as pets. Plant seeds can sneak in on the clothes and shoes of tourists. Plants and animals can travel in the water carried in ships. This water is then pumped out in ports when the ships load their cargo.

Some governments have strict laws about what people can bring into their countries. These laws can help slow down the introduction of unwanted wildlife.

▲ The octopus tree might look good in a garden, but if it gets into ecosystems where it does not belong it quickly takes over and covers everything. Even boulders are not safe! It is now a real pest in Hawaii, where it smothers indigenous forests.

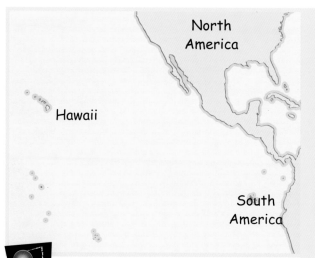

North America

Hawaii

South America

◄ Hawaii is an island. The nearest land is a long way away. Because of this location, Hawaii was not used to aliens. Scientists guess that it used to take a new species 25,000 years to reach Hawaii. Today a new plant or animal arrives there every 18 days! Hawaii might have no indigenous plants and animals left in a few years.

YOU CAN DO IT!

🐾 Do not let imported aquarium fish escape into rivers, where they can eat the indigenous fish.

🐾 If you have a pet cat, keep it inside at night to make sure it does not hunt indigenous animals.

🐾 If you have a garden, persuade your parents to plant species indigenous to your local area.

READ MORE ABOUT:

• food webs on page 7.

The richest place on Earth

Tropical rainforests are home to the greatest variety of plants and animals in our world. These hot, wet forests cover 6 percent of our world's surface. Yet they are home to nearly 70 percent of our world's wildlife.

Rainforests are being cleared for timber, farmland and mining. The wildlife is losing its habitat. The indigenous people who live in the rainforest also have to find somewhere else to live.

The tallest, oldest trees in the forest break through the canopy. This emergent layer is home to more birds, animals and lizards.

The tree branches form a roof over the forest. This is the canopy. It is crowded with birds, mammals, snakes and frogs feeding on the leaves, seeds, flowers and fruits.

The understorey is dark, gloomy and humid. Here ferns, palms and vines drip with moisture, and lizards, fruit bats and spiders search for food.

The forest floor is dark and damp. Small animals, insects, fungi and bacteria live here.

▲ A tropical rainforest supports many different habitats.

▶ The rainforests in Brazil are being cleared at an alarming rate.

STOP & THINK

Have we discovered everything that lives in the rainforest?

- **One thousand years ago, 34 percent of our world was covered in forest.**

- **Fifty years ago, 32 percent was covered in forest.**

- **Today, 12 percent is covered in forest.**

- **Every 20 seconds, 2.5 acres (1 hectare) of rainforest in Brazil is cut down. That is about a football field every two seconds.**

Hidden secrets

Many of the foods we eat, such as avocados, bananas, pineapples and some nuts, came originally from rainforests. If we did not have rainforests, we would not have chocolate or chewing gum! Rainforest plants are also used to make medicine to treat illnesses such as heart disease and cancer. Each year hundreds of new plants are discovered. If we do not act to save the rainforests, we could lose many foods and medicinal plants before we have even discovered them.

▲ When the trees go, so does the wildlife.

In the Amazon rainforest, scientists are working with the indigenous people to find out more about the rainforests and the plants and animals that live there. If we share our skills and knowledge, we can all benefit from the rainforest without destroying it.

▲ Indigenous people living in rainforests have a deep understanding of nature and wildlife. They know how to use nature without destroying it. We need to value their rights to live in the rainforest.

YOU CAN DO IT!

🐾 Reuse paper whenever you can. Be sure to write on both sides. Then recycle the paper when you are finished. Recycling one ton of paper saves about 19 trees.

🐾 Tell your parents not to buy furniture or other goods made from rainforest timber, such as mahogany or teak. Use plantation timber or second-hand timber instead.

Changing our food

All the fruit and vegetables we eat have been bred from wild plants. Since the 1970s, scientists have been working on genetically engineered food. The **cells** of all living things contain genes. Genes carry chemical information that controls how our bodies are made. By choosing a gene from one thing and adding it to the genes of another, scientists can create crops that can fight disease, grow faster or produce more. Crops can even be changed to contain medicine or more vitamins.

When more farmers use similar breeds, biodiversity is lost. In the last 20 years, the number of rice varieties grown in Sri Lanka has fallen from 2,000 to five. In India, rice varieties have dropped from 30,000 to ten.

▲ The number of rice varieties in Sri Lanka is now very small.

▶ Dolly the sheep was the first cloned mammal.

STOP & THINK

What might happen if we make more and more genetically engineered plants and animals?

One-third of livestock breeds are at the point of extinction because farmers are using only breeds that grow fast or big.

Growing monster food?

No one really knows if it is safe to take genes from one species and add them to another. No one knows what might happen if genetically engineered plants and animals mix with nature. This is one of the reasons why some people disagree with the idea of genetically engineered food.

If the climate changes, the crops we use today may not be able to survive the new conditions. Then we will need to use wild plants to help breed new crops to suit the new climate. If the wild plants are gone, there will be nothing left to use. If we try to keep plant biodiversity, then there will still be many species that will be able to survive.

▲ Seed banks store seeds for the future but they can only hold a small percentage of the total number of species.

▼ Farmers develop new breeds from wild plants. These food plants have all come from wild cabbage.

| broccoli | kale | brussels sprouts | cauliflower | cabbage | kohlrabi |

There are more than 20,000 species of edible plants in our world. We eat only 3,000 of them!

YOU CAN DO IT!

- 🐾 Be an informed consumer. Read food labels and know where your food comes from.
- 🐾 If food is not labeled where you live, write to the government and ask for labeling laws.
- 🐾 If you have a garden, grow your own vegetables. Save and reuse seeds for future planting.

READ
MORE ABOUT:

- biodiversity on page 8
- climate change on page 10.

Find out about the ecosystems where you live.

Collect animal tracks

Next time you go walking in nature, take some track-casting equipment. Then you can search for animal tracks and start your own collection.

What you need:

- plastic wrap

- a plastic ice-cream bucket

- a bottle of water

- plaster of paris

- a stick

- a box

- sandpaper.

What to do:

1. Look for animal tracks on bare, dry ground. When you find one, carefully clean off any leaves, twigs or other matter.

2. Line the track with plastic wrap. Leave some wrap sticking up over the edge of the track.

3. Tip about one cup of water into the bucket. Sprinkle on about 1 1/2 cups of plaster of paris. Use a stick to mix it together.

4. Fill the plastic-lined track with the mixture. Let it set for about 30 minutes.

5. When the plaster is hard enough, carefully lift it out with the plastic edges. Put it in the box to carry home.

6. Leave the track to harden overnight before you peel off the plastic. Then remove any bubbles or rough edges and smooth with sandpaper.

7. Find out the name of the animal that made the track and scratch the name on the bottom of the plaster.

What happens?

You can make a collection of animal tracks to learn about the wildlife that shares your ecosystem.

Here are some ways to help wildlife. After all, they are helping you by making your ecosystem rich in biodiversity!

This bath is for the birds!

What you need:

- lid from a plastic garbage can or the plastic or pottery dish from under a plant pot

- small shovel

- water.

What to do:

1. Find a good spot to place the lid or dish, which will be your bird bath. Near some trees is good. The birds can sit in a branch to check out the area for cats or other dangers before they take the plunge.

2. Dig a shallow hole. It should be just big enough to fit the bath so that it is even with the ground.

3. Fill the bath with about 2 inches (5 centimeters) of water.

4. Make sure you put in fresh water every few days.

Seed search

You might be surprised how many different types of seeds you can find in your own backyard or local park. Take a walk and see. Look for any dying flowers. As a flower dies it swells to form a fruit. The fruit then ripens and opens and the seed falls out.

Ask permission to cover a dying flower with a small plastic bag. Close the bag with a twist tie. Leave the bag until the fruit ripens. Then the seeds will fall into the bag and you can collect them.

Collect as many seeds as you can. Then plant them!

If you find a worm lost on the street, save its life by scooping it up on a leaf and moving it to a garden. The worm will help you by eating garbage and making the soil rich and airy.

Think globally

OUR WORLD

Everything in our world is connected. The animals, plants, soil, air and water are all part of the same living planet. We are part of the same planet, too. Protecting the variety of life—the biodiversity—in our world helps to keep our whole world healthy. But balancing human needs for resources with plant and animal needs for natural habitats is not easy.

▲ The World Wildlife Fund has a lot of support around the world.

Working together

Around our world people are getting together to help wildlife. The World Wildlife Fund (WWF) has a network of organizations in more than 100 countries with more than five million supporters. They are working to conserve wildlife and their habitats by focusing attention on a small number of threatened species such as giant pandas, tigers, great apes, whales, elephants and rhinos. They hope that when people learn about the threats to these popular creatures, they will also want to help other species of wildlife.

United Nations

In 1975 the Convention on International Trade in Endangered Species was set up. More than 100 countries have joined. The organization controls or bans the hunting and trade of endangered animals and plants. It has stopped most illegal fishing and whaling, as well as the sale of animal furs.

STOP & THINK

Biodiversity is being lost at such a fast rate because of the actions of people. Are we doing enough to save our world's wildlife?

Governments in action

The best way to save wildlife is to protect habitats as nature reserves and national parks, where wildlife can live in peace.

In 1992 governments from around the world met at an Earth Summit in Brazil. It was the world's biggest meeting. All the leaders at the meeting signed an agreement called Agenda 21. It is a plan for using—and looking after—our world in the 21st century. All countries could do more to keep our world healthy. The strength of Agenda 21 is that the world's leaders agreed that we need to take action.

Agenda 21: Aims for our wildlife

- Protect biodiversity.
- Identify endangered species and threats to endangered species.
- Save species from extinction.
- Preserve habitats.
- Slow global warming.
- Work with indigenous people to learn about plants and animals.
- Study and understand plants and animals.
- Use plants and animals in a sustainable way.

▲ Most countries have national parks run by the government. These areas have laws to protect the wildlife and to stop hunting and poaching.

◀ These children were part of the Earth Summit in Brazil in 1992.

YOU CAN DO iT!

- ❋ Write to politicians and tell them what you think needs to be done to protect plants and animals.
- ❋ Talk to your parents about what you can do to help plants and animals.
- ❋ Check if there are any wildlife groups, national parks, nature reserves or zoos in your area. Volunteer to help.

Sustaining our world

OUR WORLD

To survive on this planet, we need to take and use the things our world gives us. But we also need to keep all the parts of our world working in balance. Scientists call it ecologically sustainable development. It means taking only what we need from our world to live today, and at the same time keeping our world healthy so it can keep giving in the future.

Biodiversity is all around us, no matter where we live. A sustainable world is one where we conserve the whole habitat because all plants and animals rely on each other. We cannot protect a single species if its habitat is dying!

Everything in our world is connected. If we damage one part we can affect the other parts. If we look after one part, we can help protect all the other parts. The future of our world depends on our actions now.

▼ The different parts of our world are all connected.

Glossary

amphibians animals that hatch in water but later develop lungs and breathe air

carbon dioxide a gas that animals breathe out and plants take in

cells the smallest units of living matter

cloned copied exactly

consumer a person who buys or uses a product or service

developed countries countries where the way of life is based on the use of resources by industries

extinct no longer alive. This term refers to animal species, not individual animals

fertilizers substances added to the soil to make plants grow faster or bigger

fossil fuels fuels such as coal or gas that formed in Earth from the remains of animals and plants

habitats the natural homes of plants or animals

imported brought in from another country

indigenous originally living in an area

pesticides chemicals used to kill plant or animal pests

poachers people who break the law and kill an animal on someone else's land

predators animals that hunt and kill other animals for food

raw materials materials used to make something else

reservoirs lakes that form behind dams

resources things that people make use of

sewage waste carried away in sewers and drains

species any group of living things that can breed together to produce offspring

sustainable the use of resources in a way that leaves enough for others to use over a long period of time

tranquilized given a drug that keeps an animal still and calm

Index